Nimbus Publishing Limited
PO Box 9166, Halifax, NS B3K 5M8
(902) 455-4286  nimbus.ca

Printed and bound in Canada

Author photo: Raul Rincon
Illustrator photo: Richard Rudnicki

Library and Archives Canada Cataloguing in Publication

Grant, Shauntay
The city speaks in drums / Shauntay Grant ; Susan Tooke, illustrator.

ISBN 978-1-55109-758-9
ISBN 978-1-55109-766-4 (with CD)

I. Tooke, Susan  II. Title.

PS8613.R3663C57 2010   jC813'.6   C2009-907315-3

We acknowledge the financial support of the Government of Canada through the Book Publishing Industry Development Program (BPIDP) and the Canada Council, and of the Province of Nova Scotia through the Department of Tourism, Culture and Heritage for our publishing activities.

young child runs stick 'cross fence near basketball courts
    hear young brothas dribblin'
grippin' the ball with they grip
    then *pass* with a whip
whip quick 'round jerseys and then
    pull back, release, up and in
ball whips through rim

bounce twice on ground
    and sound
reverberates through air
    bounces off rec centre's brick

schoolyard kids scuffin' earth with they kicks
playin' tricks, gamin' games
runnin' up and down the block
*whip* water pistols 'round
drenchin' each other up to they necks
trigger release them water jets
*press* on **arms**
*waist* to **legs**
water beats drums 'cross they chest
no room to rest

adrenaline pumpin' like a *storm* inside they one

young childs run

callin' to each other in song

"i'm gonna catch ya!" sings one

and *one* plus *one*

laughin'

they little feet **parumpapumpum**
    like little drumma boy's drum
cross dixon field
    jet past squaretown barbecues
beneath gold rays and rainbow hues
    skies of blues

run up gottingen past joe's
round the corner at cunard street
few more blocks to the armoury
come to light and
YIELD...

...then cross to the commons field
run on earth
race 'round tree
and me
see all this
hear all this
embrace the city's vibe and
wrap myself in
her rhyme

the city's drum beats from many directions
one such: spring garden and south park intersection
man with spoons taps rhythms on the corner
passersby drop
dimes,
nickels
and quarters

down the street
homemade drum set drummer jams outside the bank
saxophones spit rhythms
singers verse licks
musicians caress the guits with precision

and just in front the library
    at the end of the street
natty dreadlocks *whip* air
    to the beat of the djembe
eardrum bound
    more music more sound
    more music more sound!

beat boxin' on the corner
songs sung 'round the way
word iz bond spittin' verses from the highlife café
what they say?
spoken word permeatin' city ways
with words, rhythms and sounds
accents and rhythms seep into selves

poppin' and lockin'
hip hoppin'
on the waterfront
the city speaks in drums
the city speaks in drums!

she verbalizes her thoughts in *english*, *french*, *italian*, *german*, *spanish*, *chinese*, *swahili*, **and** some

she dances on shingles and drums

she is a soulful singer
  her melodies linger
pressin' sweet beats on my bones
  her lyric has no form
her melodies are free
  she got **free verse** in her earth
and sound rides on her wind

she is drumfest and kuumba
pipes and drums
religious meetings and masses
music classes
latin dances
jazz and blues
international tattoos
quick beats and mellow tones